Listening to the Thunder

Listening to the Thunder

Poems by

Helen Tzagoloff

The Oliver Arts & Open Press

Copyright © 2012 by Helen Tzagoloff

All rights reserved. No part of this book may be used or reproduced in any manner without written permission from the Publisher, except in the case of brief quotations that may appear in articles and reviews.

Library of Congress Control Number: 2011929517
Tzagoloff, Helen.
Listening to the Thunder
Poetry by Helen Tzagoloff

ISBN: 978-0-9829878-0-3

I would like to thank the editors of the following publications in which these poems first appeared:

Rockhurst Review: "First Deaths," "Listening to Mozart"
California Quarterly: "Vladivostock"
The Prose Poem: An International Journal: "Mail-Order Bride"
Comstock Review: "Knowledge"
Exit 13: "Crossing the Street with a Blind Man"
Barrow Street: "Juliette"
Sing Heavenly Muse: "A Few Pointers on Preparing for a Job Interview"
Another Chicago Magazine: "Demon on Sabbatical"
Slant: "After O'Hara after Mayakovsky"
PMS: "Reunion"
The Kerf: "No Reason"
Vallum: "Traveling with Books"
The New Verse News: "Sand Is for Members"
New York Quarterly: "Things to Fear while Sleeping"
Blueline: "Listening to the Thunder"

In the sequence poem "Can't Sleep" section 1 was published in *Blueline* under the title "Berries." Section 2, under the title "Anniversary Gift" was published in the *Bay Area Poetry Coalition (BAPC)* Anthology. Section 6 was published in *Mudfish* under the title "Hospitality."

"Mail-Order Bride" was published in *The Best of the Prose Poem*: An International Journal.

"Throwing Away the Corset" won the First Place Award in the Icarus International 2002 Literary Competition and was published in the Icarus 2002 Anthology *One Small Step*.

"Ralph," "The Breakthrough," "Things to Fear while Sleeping," and "Listening to the Thunder" were published in the Interpoezia Anthology, *Stranger at Home (Interpoezia* and Numina Press).

For encouragement and feedback on my writing, I am grateful to Nancy Flaun Green and Nicole Andonov and to my husband Alex, always my first reader. I am grateful to Elaine Equi and Phillis Levin for their instruction and encouragement. Special gratitude to Molly Peacock and Eric Larsen for reading and rereading many of the poems in this book and for their editorial assistance.

The Oliver Arts & Open Press
2578 Broadway (Suite #102)
New York, NY 10025
http://www.oliveropenpress.com

For Virgil, Bayard, James,
Wesley and Catherine

CONTENTS

Foreword 9

I

My Most Memorable Bath 13
First Deaths 14
Before Ballpoint Pens or How I Came to Be 17
Vladivostock 18

II

Coming to America 21
Ralph 22
Eyevengo 23
Boris' Dreams 25
Mail-Order Bride 26
Motel on Route 9 27

III

The Breakthrough 31
Zoya 33
Gifts 35
Babysitting 37
Senior Year 39

IV

Kate 43
Grisha's Restaurant 44
February 46
Nocturnal Episode 47
Friday Night 49

V

Can't Sleep 53
Listening to Mozart 58
Knowledge 59
Crossing the Street with a Blind Man 60
Mr. Bologh Answers My Question 61
Juliette 63
Meeting a College Classmate 64

My Mother Tells Me Her Dream 66
A Few Pointers on Preparing for a Job Interview 67
Demon on Sabbatical 68
After O'Hara after Mayakovsky 70
Reunion 72
Remembering My Father 73

VI

Longing 77
Nachtkerze 78
When I Step Outside 80
Throwing away the Corset 81
July 82
Flying from Rome 83
No Reason 84
Traveling with Books 85

VII

Dirt 89
My Bare Elbows 91
Intensive Care Unit 93
Omaha Beach 95
Dream with Cardboard Suitcase 96
Do You Know Who Your Neighbors Are? 98
Sand Is for Members 101
Attack in Tarrytown 103
Things to Fear while Sleeping 105
The Passing Car 106
On a Train Along the Hudson River. 108
Listening to the Thunder 110

FOREWORD

Helen Tzagoloff is a Russian-born American poet who has lived most of her life in the United States. She is an example of a writer with mixed sensibilities: those of an American and of a "genetically" Russian with a childhood rooted in Russia. Listening to the Thunder is unusual both in its artistic approach and subject matter that recalls the author's childhood memories of the Second World War and of the hardships endured by her parents and relatives during that tumultuous period. These early recollections are juxtaposed with the later experiences in the United States. An illustrative example is the excellent title poem:

> When it thundered, mother
> would draw the drapes, sit silently
> away from the windows.
>
> *   *   *
>
> When I hear thunder, I turn off
> the computer, sit on the sofa, drink
> coffee and listen to the thunder.

A poet's emotional reservoir is shaped by his or her social milieu and cultural idiom while poetic tension remains tightly linked to the native language. Helen Tzagoloff's native language is both Russian and English, the latter naturally acquired in the course of her intellectual growth and development. Even the titles of her poems signal the transition from events in her childhood to scenes of American everyday life: "The Most Memorable Bath," "First Deaths," "Vladivostok," "Coming to America," "Motel on Route 9," "Intensive Care Unit," "Omaha Beach," "Attack in Tarrytown," and "On a Train along the Hudson River."

A good poem is a representation of direct speech, a personal communication, in a metaphorical form. And this is precisely what is magically achieved in this collection of poems that constitute life stories transmitted in personal yet distanced ways. The poems are never merely cerebral metaphors. Living with a new language requires a range of complex adjustments. The language becomes not simply a tool for survival but also a second self (alter ego), one that is radically different from the still-existing first self, inevitably created by one's native language. Helen Tzagoloff is an American in all respects with a soul reflecting a strange and complex blend of sensibilities that act as a fountain for these interesting, piercing and at the same time subtle poems that range from descriptive, nostalgic remembrances of events spanning a lifetime.

The writing is that of an established poet with a secure command of a rich and yet not over used poetic language. One of my favorite longer, descriptive poems "First Deaths," is from the author's childhood years, though she is also a master of the short, tight and philosophical ("No Reason") as well as psychological and contemplative poem ("Listening to Mozart"). Many of the pieces are interesting short stories with palpably live characters and situations.

The narrative emphasis in some poems ("Babysitting" or "Grisha's Restaurant") is not so much on the actual occurrence but rather on a surprising interpretation of an event as it filters through the prism of the author's imagination. Whatever the genre, these poems achieve unexpected and rewarding aesthetic effects. Reading them is like looking through a vivid and truthful photographic album of an entire life.

Andrey Gritsman, 2011

Andrey Gritsman is the author of the poetry collections *Long Fall* (Spuyten Duyvil Press, New York) and, most recently, *Live Landscape* (Červená Barva Press, Boston).

I

MY MOST MEMORABLE BATH

Cold Russian winter.
The Germans may be here tomorrow
in our village south of Moscow.
My grandmother, tall, thin, her gray hair
in a braid, is giving four grandchildren
a bath inside a stone wood-burning stove
used for baking, cooking and heating
her one-room hut. Because I am the thinnest
and have neither lice nor fleas,
I'm the last one to climb inside the tub
of the thrice-used water.
(In hindsight my grandmother's reasoning
doesn't make sense.)
I diligently pass the sliver of soap
over my body. I like sitting
in this small, enclosed warm place.
The water is barely tepid
when I'm told to come out.
I emerge to laughter and finger pointing.
My grandmother shakes her head,
makes me stand naked in the cold
while she wipes the soot off my back.

FIRST DEATHS

I woke from cries, long, low-pitched, monotonous.
A dog mourned the death of his master, my grandmother said.
An old man died peacefully; his body washed, dressed,
coins placed on his lids, ready for burial in the morning.
His dog, his companion, was spending the night in the house.
"Nothing to be afraid of," my grandmother said,
stroking my hair and covering me with a blanket.
"The man who died, he won't be able to feed his dog?"
I asked. "No." "Who will take care of him?
Can we bring him home?" "Relatives will care for him.
He will have a good home."

Falling asleep I listened to the dog's sad cries,
which turned to whimpers at daybreak, then stopped.

* * *

The advancing German Army bypassed the village
where I stayed with my grandmother.
In the spring when the Oka flooded over,
the villagers became conscious of their luck –
the river brought corpses floating up
from the city of Orel. Bodies of young men
in Russian or German uniforms washed ashore.

The war was not comprehensible to me.
During bombings my cousins and I would run
from window to window, watching

the exploding bursts of fire, until some adult
would shout at us to hurry to the underground shelter.

Bewildered and terrified, I watched the local women
pick up and turn the bodies to drain them of water
before dragging them away.

* * *

On our way to the train station from the market in Malahovka,
where my mother sold a pair of my father's shoes for groceries,
we passed a man crying: "Christa radee, oubeyti meynia!"
(For Christ's sake, kill me!) The man lay legless and armless
on his back on a bench in a barren muddy park.
"Why was the man like that?" "Why didn't anyone help him?"
"Didn't he have a family?" I asked my mother,
who pulled me roughly along, not answering.
I kept repeating my questions, until she yelled at me to stop.

Decades later I read that after the victory,
the country was full of men missing some or all of their limbs.
Labeled "the samovars," they congregated on skateboards,
cursing, accosting passersby, bumming cigarettes,
trying to hurt each other. These men, decorated veterans,
heroes of the Motherland, on Stalin's orders,
in the name of compassion, were sent to live out
their lives in remote deserted places.
The country could not move forward with
such reminders of the war.

* * *

Three boys and a girl, my fellow-kindergarteners,
discovered a dormant bomb buried in last year's pile of leaves.
Sereja, who held the bomb, was killed instantly. Slava died
on the way to the hospital. Alyosha lost his legs. Mira became deaf.

We were hastily fed, herded into beds and commanded
to take a nap. The children sobbed, asked for their mothers,
kept getting up. I lay still, eyes closed. Our teachers
pointed at me: "Why don't you behave like Lenochka!
See how quietly she is lying!"

I tried to understand what happened as I lay in that large
sunny room full of crying children. I knew
if I opened my eyes I would see out the window
Sereja, an oblong mound covered with a grey blanket.
How could I never see Slava?
(The teachers did not try to hide anything from us and
told us that he died on the way to the hospital.)
Earlier in the year Slava announced to the class that
he wanted to marry me. Lively, mischievous, popular,
he was good at inventing and organizing games.
His courtship consisted of sitting next to me at meals
and story times. I did not object – I think he may have been
my first love. We often played together, but on that day
I stayed inside, deciphering words in a picture book.

In the evening I watched Sereja's mother cry,
lying on the grass, pounding the earth with her fists.
Mother and several other women tried to console her.
She had to pull herself together. She had a younger child to live for.
Later they decided to leave her alone, let her cry herself out.
She cried all night. I listened as her cries got weaker and weaker.
In the morning she went to work, silent, dry-eyed.

BEFORE BALLPOINT PENS OR HOW I CAME TO BE

Claudia was dreamily walking up the stairs
to her class on Pushkin. Michael, not wanting
to be late, was running down the stairs.
They collided. Michael's inkwell flew out
in a spray of blue over Claudia's white blouse.

She was upset, but not too upset, though she owned
only two blouses. She'd been wanting to meet the tall,
blond mathematics major. Michael apologized,
offered to pay for the blouse. Claudia refused.
She soaked and scrubbed the blouse until the stains
were very faint, then dyed it deep lavender,
to compliment her chestnut brown hair and hazel eyes.

They were married at the City Registrar's Office.
Friends and classmates came to their one-room apartment
with plates and forks, gifts of food and drink.
The party spilled into the hallway where they sang
and danced to a balalaika. The neighbors joined in.

A year later, a hairless, toothless, very short person
joined Claudia and Michael in their room. This person
hardly ever slept, had no manners, no social graces and,
despite a negligible occupation of space (a laundry basket
was sufficient), demanded an extraordinary amount of attention,
which Claudia and Michael bestowed lavishly and unstintingly.

VLADIVOSTOCK

On this trip across Siberia my parents
threw a blanket over my pajamas, held me
to the window—*You must not miss
the River Lena, your namesake—Wake up!
Look at the waters of Lake Baikal!*

The monotony, the blackness of the plains
lulled me—nobody kept me awake,
but when lights appeared in the distance
I was startled—I'd grown used to blackouts,
drapes over windows, towels under doors.

I was not the only one who took note.
Everyone on the train was up, shouting:
*Look at those lights! What a sight!
The sons of bitches, they've never felt the war!*

II

COMING TO AMERICA

I breathe in the raw fresh air, a relief
from the staleness of our cabin where
my mother has lain sick for twenty-one days.

I slide on the wet deck kept clean
by intermittent squalls and waves
that leap and break overboard.

We are crossing the Pacific Ocean
in mid-December. I'm eight,
the only child on the ship,

allowed to roam as I please.
This journey will be the beginning
of my lifelong love of the ocean.

My father calls my name,
hands me two lemons the cook
has given him for my mother–

sucking on them will help her.
"And change your clothes,
you're completely drenched."

I leave him to stay alone, watching
the waves crest, listening to the wind,
wondering how it will be in America.

RALPH

"Americans are in a hurry,"
was the reason my father-in-law gave
for choosing Ralph as his name.

He shed the patronymic
on the subway ride after Ellis Island.
The immigration officer had already
trimmed the surname, removing a consonant
at the beginning and a vowel at the end.

"In America, time is money,"
instructed his sponsor.
"People have no patience
for Afanasiy Konstantinovich.
They'll reduce your name to Aff."

By his first job,
assembling brooms and mops,
he had decided on Ralph.
Quick, easy, memorable and
surprisingly not common.

It served him well, especially when
he moved up to position of office manager
at the age of fifty five.
"Just call me Ralph," he'd tell
the secretaries, the R, rolling, distinct,
not quite American.

EYEVENGO

What was the last book you've read? asked Mr. Connors
in freshman English.
Eyevengo.
Who was the author?
Vallter Skot.
Eyevengo by Vallter Skot, I repeated.

The teacher, a middle-aged man in horn-rimmed glasses,
rumpled his sparse grey hair, concentrating.
The writer is very famous, English. Also British, I added.

Red hot from embarrassment, I was afraid that Mr. Connors,
despite my fine display of knowledge of English grammar,
would say: *Sorry, your English is not good enough
to be in the Freshman class at Thomas Jefferson High School.*

Earlier he had asked the class the proper grammatical form
for the third person singular negative contraction of "to know."
Two people answered: *He don't know.*
He doesn't know, I astonished Mr. Connors, hastening to inform him
I had studied English as a foreign language.
*This is a perfect example of foreigners knowing English grammar
better than American students. They take time out to learn
correct grammar from the beginning,* he announced.

And then Eyevengo. He wanted to show me off
further to the class. Instead I failed.

Ivanhoe, by Walter Scott! exclaimed Mr. Connors,
pulling on his hair.

A horrible thought: What if I'm asked to describe the plot?
Rowena and Ivanhoe in love, her father disapproving,
knights, kidnappings, Rebecca at the stake,
Robin Hood, the noble thief, something about
Normans and Saxons that I had mostly skipped.
No, I wouldn't be able to describe the plot.

Mr. Connors went back to points of grammar,
leaving me alone. I vowed to reread Ivanhoe,
not in Russian, but in English. I would pay
careful attention to the Norman-Saxon strife.

But soon the movie came out with Elizabeth Taylor
and Robert Taylor, everyone speaking in English,
the plot clearly presented. I felt I had revisited the book.
Maybe I'll reread it in my old age. Not now.

BORIS' DREAMS

1

Boris, looking through tinted glasses, legs crossed in a movie
director's chair, a tall cool drink in one hand, in the other
a cigarette in an amber holder, is saying to a shy young actress:
"Give me your best, darling! I know you can do it!"

2

A buyer is offering a great deal of money for a valuable article
—a lost painting, an ancient text, a pre-revolutionary rifle—
that has come into Boris's possession.

3

Boris, in a linen jacket, with a silk, loosely knotted ascot tie,
is at the roulette table in Monte Carlo, playing for high stakes.
He is married to a wealthy, beautiful woman, twenty years younger,
who is mad about him.

4

At Meg's Coffee Shop where Boris works as a waiter, the owner calls
for him to pick up the phone. The workers are not supposed to get
personal calls during the lunch rush hour. The owner is watching him
with unconcealed animosity. On the other end, an attorney is informing
Boris he has inherited a million dollars.

MAIL-ORDER BRIDE

He had many responsibilities—dinners with elderly mother, tennis on Saturdays. Didn't she want him to be fit? Drinks with the boss, that's how it is in America, if you want to advance.

At breakfast he read the newspaper. In the evening they watched snatches of shows on television. "Such junk," he declared, switching channels. She longed for conversation and tea with fragrant, old-world bread. "I'd like to have a baby," she told him. "Let's wait. Maybe I'm too old. This is such a nice life," he said.

When she became a citizen, she moved to a one-room basement apartment, found a job in a nursing home. Some said she was selfish and calculating.

MOTEL ON ROUTE 9

The woman with varicose veins,
in a gray dress, white frilly apron,

cleaning toilet bowls, stripping beds,
hoping for a tip by the bedside lamp,

grew up with a view of snow-capped
mountains, swam in a clear deep lake,

dreamed of becoming a great ballerina.

III

THE BREAKTHROUGH

2 a.m., Sunday I open the door,
take off my shoes and walk up the stairs.
In my hand are two dollars.
My first job, babysitting for the neighbors.

The only light, a lit cigarette.
My father is downstairs by the window.
I hope he doesn't see me. There is a lot
on his mind. He doesn't have a job.
Some people say he's not well.

"It's not really like working. In America
all teenage girls babysit," I begged.
"Go," my mother said, exasperated.
"Don't mention this to your father.
I'll tell him myself," she added
matter-of-factly, as if it's too
insignificant a matter to bother him with.

I'm the only girl in High School with hair
in braids. The only girl who doesn't wear lipstick.
My greatest wish is to be like everyone else,
but when I answer a question (I never volunteer),
it becomes so quiet in the room, I know I'm foreign.
I wish I could disappear and never come back.

At the top of the stairs as I'm about
to breathe out the breath I've been holding,
my father says: "It's been hard for us, but not

so hard that a child of mine has to work
late into the night." He sounds resigned, defeated.
I stand in silence. He lights a cigarette.
"You better go to bed."

ZOYA

She did as she promised, showing photos of me, looking like a prehistoric reptilian bird, arms flapping, palms magnified, gigantic 5-digit claws poised to pounce, hair curlers in iguana-like crests. Zoya had appeared unexpectedly, clicking her camera—she fancied herself the future famous photographer specializing in realism—while I was out in the backyard, watching my brother and sister. "Prize winning! Caught with your pants down!" she laughed.

She passed around the pictures at her 16th Birthday Party to her sophisticated San Francisco friends who barely glanced at them, being as always engaged in political talk.

It was a happy day for me when Zoya enrolled in my school. Someone to share the unwelcome spotlight—another student from behind the Iron Curtain to question. And such curiosity my presence engendered in this small town High School in 1951! The questions ranged from seeking an explanation for the Balkan crisis to asking if Russian girls got periods. The never ending disbelief: You don't look Russian! I did not look like the photos of Russian women sweeping the streets the C.I.A. propaganda machine generated. (They must use searchlights in broad daylight to find such ugly examples, the émigrés joked.) I was sure I had Swedish and Asian ancestors, I said. The Varangians from the North, the centuries of Genghis Khan.

I introduced Zoya to the two shy girls I ate lunch with. Emily, whose family spent the war interred in a special camp for those of Japanese origin, and Myra from a large family. Right away Zoya made fun of my friends. Emily was bowlegged. Myra looked pregnant in an oversize coat, a hand-me-down from her mother.

She insisted on speaking only in Russian. I was uncomfortable, would try to translate. It was easier to become isolated. Not wise, I vaguely sensed, but I longed for companionship with someone of my background, someone who had experienced the war. And Zoya brought fun into my life at a time when my family was troubled. I met her friends in San Francisco, went on trips, parties, picnics. Her friends were continually striving to preserve our Russianness. We played Russian music, read Russian poetry, put on Russian plays for a Russian audience, formed an all-Russian Scout Troup. We reminded ourselves that one day we would return to our Great Mother Russia. We must not become Americanized.

On Monday after the party I skipped lunch to study for an exam—fortunately Zoya and I attended different classes. After school I stayed behind—claiming to have a conference. The break was not easy. Zoya excluded me from social events, threatened to reveal the real name my parents had changed for political reasons, made fun of my appearance—easy to do, since like Myra, I dressed in second-hand clothing.

One day toward the end of our Junior year, she asked to walk home with me. She told me her parents had arranged for her to live with a Russian family in San Francisco. She was leaving next week. I was shocked, but she believed it would be for the best. She was unhappy, needed her Russian friends. I felt I had let her down. I think we could've become good friends after that last walk. I didn't know it then, but my own family, too, soon moved to the opposite side of the country.

GIFTS

for Natasha and Lydia

1

The star of the useless things
in the trunk is a stole, a silver
and white net of seashells of yarn,
the colors still bright, the fringe even.
Where could one wear such a fancy item?

This question was not on my mind
as I deciphered: *yarn over,*
slip under, pick up below–
the salesclerk had warned the pattern
was not for beginners.
I knit in secret after school–
a birthday surprise for my mother.
I pictured her happy, glamorous,
protected from the cold seeping in
through windows and doors.

The stole will be useful, much worn.
It will not lie flat, stowed away
in a drawer. Guaranteed to be
wrinkle-free, moth-proof, of such
strength, it will last forever.
In years to come, Orlon freed
women of the drudgery
of sewing up seams constantly
ripping apart, but I learned

of its strength when my teeth
failed to serve me as scissors.

My mother, displaced from her home,
supporting her children alone,
too proud to ask for help, ashamed
of her imperfect English,
led a life of few social functions.
She did not wear my stole.

2

I sat by the iced-over window
embroidering in dim light.
My mother walked in silently,
bringing a lamp. She worried
I was damaging my eyesight.
She worried that a sudden noise
would cause me to bite my tongue,
maim my face. I was intent, forcing
through fabric an oversize needle,
pulling up thread a yard long.
When startled I sometimes jumped,
waving the needle close to my face.

Using a ruler I copied
an old Ukrainian design on
linen cut out for the apron–
a birthday gift for my mother.
The design in a criss-cross stitch
was in red and black, red for
the roses, black for the stems and leaves.

My handiwork was proudly displayed
to relatives and friends. Amazing,
they said, for a seven-year-old.

The apron was placed in a trunk.
She'll wear it when my father returns
from the front, my mother assured me.
We soon left our home, taking few
  things, the apron not among them.

BABYSITTING

I smoke a cigarette, listen
to the Hit Parade on TV.
Both a treat. We don't own a TV.
I smoke only when babysitting
and on dates between dancing,
while sipping a tall Tom Collins.

In the bathroom I examine
the powder, the lipstick, eye shadow.
Lots of girls try on makeup. I don't.
And I don't eat on babysitting jobs.
I just have the one cigarette.
My employers discreetly leave
an opened pack. This is the fifties.
Everyone smokes. There are lots of babies.

A flimsy pink nightgown on the back of
the bathroom door smells of lotion,
perfume and human odor I'm not sure of.
Also a rubber water bottle that has
instead of a stopper at the bottom,
a piece of hard tubing with holes at the end.

I'm babysitting for a man who is taking
his helper out to a movie.
Wendy, friend of the family, helps with
the two children, a one-year old and
a two-year old, while the wife works
as a nurse the late shift.

After the children have been put to bed,
the husband and Wendy sit outside,
smoking, drinking, laughing. I know this
because we live across the street.

I hardly ever see the wife. She works
overtime, the family's sole support,
while her husband, a Korean War veteran,
attends college on the G.I. Bill.
I feel restless, turn off the TV,
smoke another cigarette. A mistake—now
I don't feel well. I've done my homework,
finished reading *Of Mice and Men*.

Walking around, I spot on the kitchen counter
next to *Joy of Cooking*, a small leather-bound
notebook. The cover inscribed "Diary."
On the first page: *I love Jimmy so*.
The only sentence.

My employer and Wendy arrive. It takes
Jimmy awhile to multiply 35 cents by four.
He and Wendy are very tipsy. I collect
the dollar forty, say good night.
Outside I can hear them laughing.
They still have an hour before
the wife comes home.

SENIOR YEAR

We danced the rumba, samba, cha-cha-cha,
"The Kiss of Fire" tango and sang along to
"Guantanamera, yo soy un hombre sincero."
In a lull between records, Pietro took my hand
and said: "I want to show you my family photographs."

We went inside the bedroom and looked
at an album of photographs. Pietro played
a tape recording from his mother in Argentina.
It was in Spanish, but he translated it for me.
His mother expressed the usual concerns
about her son's health and welfare.
Was he eating properly? Did he dress warmly,
wear galoshes in the rain, a scarf and earmuffs
in cold, windy weather?
Was he taking the vitamins she had sent him?

"You must be a virgin," Pietro said. "That's a shame,"
he sighed and kissed me. I kissed him back.
"What a sweet kiss, I'll always remember it," he said.
We went back into the living room
and another couple went inside the vacated bedroom.

"I want to see you again," Pietro said, driving me home.
"Not to sit in a dark movie house or dance
to the jukebox, but to make love. Most men wouldn't want
to bother with a virgin, but I find you so attractive,
I'm willing to be your first man.

There will always be a man who desires you,
but you'll remember me as your first.
And I'll remember you for trusting me to be your first,
a memory I will treasure."
He kissed me and I kissed him back.
"Goodnight," I said and got out of the car.

IV

KATE

I see Kate limping, dragging
the reed-thin leg encased in metal
behind its mate,
along the icy pavement.

Her boy-friend, the only man
who's asked her for a date,
waits by the car—red-faced,
smiling broadly, coat wide open
in freezing rain. I am certain
the bulge in the hip pocket is a flask.

She has never been so happy,
she told me. "Do you think
a man could love me as I am?"
The question took me by surprise.
I don't remember how I answered.

We'd been meeting for lunch
for four years. Not once did she
speak of her handicap, nor did we
ever mention polio.

We watched them drive off very fast.
Then we headed for Meltzer's Deli
for pastrami sandwiches.
Sandra said: "This will not last.
He's using her."

GRISHA'S RESTAURANT

When Grisha got angry he threw dishes
against the wall. I had never seen dishes
smashed except in James Cagney movies.
It scared me, violence in the boss,
owner of Gregory's Restaurant, a popular
campus eatery where I'd just gotten
a part-time waitressing job.

"You're complaining about meatloaf!
Ungrateful good-for-nothings, I give you
nutritious, homemade food prepared
by Tsar's Royalty! You want steak?
You see me eating steak?" Grisha thundered.

An outburst in response to Nick's
sighing: "Meatloaf again!"
"Don't worry," Nick whispered to me
between forkfuls of meatloaf and mashed
potatoes, "Grisha breaks plates
that are already cracked or chipped."

I'd become tired of operating the addressograph
at the Alumni Office. "Get a job at Grisha's,"
Nick had suggested. "He's not a bad boss,
and the customers, our fellow students
are not demanding."

"Any special way I should dress?" I asked
after the interview. "Naked. I would prefer
my waitresses to be naked," Grisha dismissed me.

There were two other waitresses, long-legged
Estonian blondes and three Russian guys,
all part-time, all students, all recently arrived DP's
as were Grisha himself and his wife Olga,
who sat glued to the cash register
fourteen hours a day, seven days a week.

The Tsar's Royalty, a man in his sixties,
came to work dressed in a suit and tie,
chain-smoking while he cooked, the cigarette
in a dark amber holder, the ash growing,

falling into whatever he was stirring,
sometimes like an arrow hitting the bullseye,
smack in the center of one of the circles of grease
swimming in that day's soup of the day.

Grisha never yelled at the Royalty chef,
treated him with the utmost politeness,
never mentioned the ash.
At first I made excuses, wouldn't eat at the restaurant.
Grisha even once commented: "Rich, shunning
the benefit I offer out of the goodness of my heart.
Good. More money for me."

When I finally overcame my reluctance,
I discovered I liked meatloaf and mashed potatoes.

FEBRUARY

Snow drifts rise, ghosts
laughing, screaming,
sunken chests, club
feet, swollen bellies.

I shiver, numb,
swallow burning wind
and car exhaust fumes.
I wait in the dusk
for the city bus
to take me to my home
on Fish Hatchery Road.

NOCTURNAL EPISODE

Do you hear someone moaning? I ask Ronnie.
He's strumming on his guitar, searching for
chords to *Sixteen tons and what do you get?
Another day older and deeper in debt!*

It's two thirty in the morning.
There are just the two of us in the apartment
we share on 113th Street. Our other apartment mate,
Nancy, is sleeping over at her boyfriend's place.

No, he interjects between *tons* and *and*.
The moans are becoming louder. I think I hear
knocking on the wall. *We must go next door.
Someone may be hurt,* I insist, afraid to go alone.

He's annoyed, but gives in. *Probably a cat in heat.
We're going to make a nuisance of ourselves!*
We pound and pound on the door.
At last a man's face appears behind a chain.

He's hard of hearing, keeps shouting, *What's
the problem?* cupping his ears elephant-style
as we shout about the moans–
his seventy-year-old sister has fallen, breaking a hip.

When she returns from the hospital
she tells the neighbors Ronnie has saved her life.
She gives him a Grand Marnier torte from *Dumas*.
Ronnie is very pleased with this gift.
He takes the torte to his girlfriend in Larchmont
where they eat it the following day on her birthday.

FRIDAY NIGHT

I'm rubbing my eyes dry, biting
my lips to the point of bleeding.
The phone is not ringing, there is
no buzzing on the intercom.

I'm yes'ing and no'ing the windows,
the paintings, the rugs. He's coming,
he's not coming. This is absurd.
How dare you stand me up, vermin,

cheating crocodile! I'm not some
sweet little thing to do your bidding,
a meek mouse you can push into
a corner whenever you please.

Eleven o'clock. If you come now,
I will not answer the buzzer.
I'm not going to wait anymore!
I'm tossing the red silk dress

I just bought into the closet—
kick off the black suede pumps,
scrub away the perfume you gave me.
I'm going to bed and think of eternity.

       * * *

Still on the yes and no game
I'm wasting time, *ad nauseam*

playing solitaire. He will phone,
he won't phone. The buzzer rings.

"You're twenty four hours late," I say
calmly laying out the cards.
He protests, the date is tonight.
He keeps protesting. He's beginning

to sound sincere. I'm engrossed
in the cards. He stops talking.
It becomes very quiet.
Maybe he's left. I may start crying.

He touches my hair. I turn around.
There is nothing to forgive. I choose
to believe. I don't want to sit
alone playing solitaire when

there's a man wishing to take me out,
expostulate on Engels and Marx,
show me a good time in my red dress,
a touch of Arpege behind my ears.

V

CAN'T SLEEP

1

Didn't you notice:
It's summer,
season of gooseberries,
blackberries, blueberries.
Go out, stay away
from poison ivy,
ticks and snakes,
bring in the crops,
then lie down
here with me
on the blue sofa
with red pillows.

2

An antique amber pendant,
reddish dark brown
like the blood of my love.

Inside a petrified insect
almost intact,
a spider of doubt and deceit
patiently waiting.

3

As I entered the room,
he pretended he did not see me.

Later introducing me
to his wife, he watched me
intently, as he told her,
he and I went to college together.
He spoke slowly, measuring out
each word, as if there had been
something between us.

When he came up to me while
I stood alone, and leaned
toward me, asking how I have been,
I saw his wife watching and knew
he knew she was watching.

We didn't talk long.
She felt a cold coming on,
wished to go home.
He looked pleased as he put his arm
protectively around her waist.

4

I don't understand,
so often I prayed for release,
for his death, yes, death,
and now I can't sleep.
I lie awake and stare
at the ceiling.
I don't feel guilty.
I did all I could,
worked hard, took care
of him, the kids.
Shiftless drunk,
couldn't hold down a job.
People warned me.
He was so handsome.

5

You are decent, reliable,
good-looking, smart.
I attract and intrigue you.
But what can I do,
when I see you
my heart doesn't stop.

6

You say your love
for another does not
diminish your love
for me, and it's love
we're talking about,
not boredom or lust.
What can you do,
the women find you
attractive, you have
a big heart.

7

She was always
quoting her husband.
He was brilliant, witty.
She was never lonely
or bored.

When he lost his job,
and after a long
search found one
in a different state,
she said she couldn't
be without her friends.

She remarried and continued
to interject the old witticisms,
embarrassing friends,
until she and her new
husband moved away.

8

She knew he had been
seeing a therapist,
but after six years
of marriage, she was
getting impatient.

Did he have to go there
five times a week?

It was expensive.
In the evenings he had
nothing to talk about.
She was right, he agreed.
But he just could not stop.

9

I lie awake
listening,
the door unchained.

You will not come,
you will come,
please come.

Familiar, dear,
in the dark
heart breaking.

Arms and legs,
soft, hard.
Don't speak.

10

Does somebody love me?
I don't know.
Do I like the idea of
somebody loving me?

I like the idea

11

We walked along the river.
You talked about your courses,
the funny things the professors said.
I smiled. The river was quiet.
The moon floated in and out of the clouds.
A man walking a black poodle said hello.
Our hands touched, my left in your right.
You stopped talking. I forgot to breathe.

LISTENING TO MOZART

The musicians are warming up,
    my ears tuning in.
Lights are dimmed.
    The conductor raises his baton.

I am listening to my father
    acting out Red Riding Hood,
swallowing air, almost crying,
    assuring myself all will end well.

My mother is struggling
    with a large satin bow
in my soft limp hair, smoothing over
    the red velvet dress.

I am dancing cheek to cheek,
    inhaling wool and tobacco,
hearing heartbeat,
    feeling very warm.

I am holding a towel.
    In my arms, a warm small body
leans on my shoulder
    and gives me a noisy wet kiss.

It is snowing. People rush home
    to escape the storm.
Snowflakes, transient and shapeless,
    turn to water on coats and hats.

KNOWLEDGE

A muffled noise
wakes me in the night.
Feet slippered or bare
hurry across the floor.
Quickly the quiet returns.
I lie, eyes open
and know someone has died.

I wait for the sirens,
for more sounds to resume.
Drifting back into sleep,
I think: There is no need
to rush. There is no emergency.

A well-known art dealer
on the floor above
suffered a fatal heart attack,
a neighbor tells me in the morning.

CROSSING THE STREET WITH A BLIND MAN

I was waiting for the light to change
with my two children I'd picked up

after school, when a blind man
asked me to help him across.

I said, sure, taking his arm.
The four of us walked across,

blind man on the right,
two kids holding on on the left.

The blind man made conversation.
How old were my children and

where did they go to school?
I told him I was tired of running

around, taking the children places.
I just couldn't wait until the day

they could cross the street on their own.
Be patient awhile longer, he told me.

MR. BOLOGH ANSWERS MY QUESTION

Mr. Bologh, our Hungarian super, stopped
fixing the faucet and thought.
I could see he was a one-job-at-a-time man.
I had asked if he knew of any children
my daughter's age in the building.

"There's a boy in the building across the street.
I know the family, do special jobs for them.
The mother is older. I think he was
a change-of-life baby. You know things are not
regular at the beginning of menopause."

I was thirty two. Menopause was not
something I thought about.

"Yes, the child must've been an accident.
Probably they couldn't have children
when young or didn't want any.
Didn't take precautions, thought it was safe."

Did Mr. Bologh feel comfortable discussing
a highly personal female subject
because I was wearing a miniskirt?

"The boy seems normal, a little quiet."
Mr. Bologh's light blue eyes greatly magnified
by thick lenses looked seriously at me.

Did he think I was hesitating, afraid
the boy might be strange because not conceived
at the peak of human fertility?

"I'm sure he's a fine boy. I was hoping for someone
in the building, a playmate for a rainy day."
That was the truth.

JULIETTE

I have trouble picturing
Juliette with a baby–
exhausted, hair dull, unwashed,
in an old robe, longing for sleep.

In a large mirrored room,
she's practicing the five positions,
warming up with pliés; her narrow
body in a black leotard,
brown hair pinned back.
How serious she was,
how she wanted to be a ballerina.

I used to pick up my daughter
after class and for a few minutes
I would stand, admiring Juliette,
the beautiful curve of her
long thin neck.

MEETING A COLLEGE CLASSMATE

I was working in a laboratory in Wisconsin.
He came to sell glassware.
"You went to Syracuse?" I asked.
"Yes, how did you know?"
"You were in some classes with me.
General Chemistry and English
in our freshman year."

"Chemistry, Monday, Wednesday, Friday
at 10? We graduated the same year?" "Yes."
"What sorority did you belong to?"
"I didn't join a sorority."
"You didn't! How could you not have
been in a sorority! I belonged to Kappa Epsilon
and married a girl from Delta Gamma.
I can't believe I don't remember you."
"Oh well, that's how it is."
"And ten years later you recognized me!"
"You haven't changed at all."
He hadn't. Tall and lanky, he looked like
a cross between William Holden and James Stewart.

"I'm amazed you weren't in a sorority.
All my best memories of college are of the fun
I had belonging to a fraternity. My greatest regret
is that I have no time for get-togethers
with my brothers, but with two children and
a third on the way, I have to work hard."

"How was it not being in a sorority?" he asked on the way out, leaving two catalogues behind.
"I managed. There were others like me."
"I still can't believe I don't remember you," he said, shaking my hand.

MY MOTHER TELLS ME HER DREAM

I was sixteen or seventeen, tanned and dark-haired.
A group of us sat on the grass.
It was a cool summer evening and I felt pleasantly tired,
with the kind of tiredness I'd feel
after a day's work in the fields. I think I even
smelled hay. I'm not sure who the other people were.
My sister Elizaveta was there and maybe my brother Piotr,
though that doesn't make sense. He was killed
in the First World War when I was six.
Everybody was talking, joking, flirting. In the distance
an owl was hooting. One of the men started to play
on the accordion an old Russian melody: *Steppe,
da steppe kroogom,* the sad song about the steppes where
a traveler loses his way and freezes to death.
When I woke up, I didn't know where I was.
When I remembered, my first thought was: *I'm going
to get up, go outside, and I won't be hearing the language
of my childhood. I'll always be a stranger here.*

A FEW POINTERS ON PREPARING FOR A JOB INTERVIEW

Shake hands firmly, but not
too firmly. Make certain your
hand is warm. Plunge into hot water
before the interview if necessary.
And make sure your nails are absolutely
clean. Please, no hint of grime.
Look serious, but smile quickly, easily,
briefly. (First cap front teeth if necessary.)
To question, what is your strongest point?
say, it is working too hard, getting carried away,
forgetting time.
To question, what is your weakest point?
say, it is working too hard, getting carried away,
forgetting time.
Be well-groomed, but a little dowdy;
dress in shades of grey.
Look intelligent, but
low-keyed and unthreatening.
If you're asked whether you plan
to have children, say that
there are already many unwanted children
in this world.
And if you're asked why you want
to work here, say that
Shmulkin, Friedken and Smith are held
in the highest esteem in the community
and you would feel privileged to work
for such a well-known and reputable firm.

DEMON ON SABBATICAL

Demon Marguerite, a whiplash administrative assistant in purgatory, chooses to spend her sabbatical in Lurabelle Murphy's womb. (Are you surprised that there are female demons? You shouldn't be. Purgatory is an Equal Opportunity Employer. It encourages applications from aboriginal persons, disabled persons, members of visible minorities, and women.)

Lurabelle Murphy is a very shy, very scared young thing. At social functions she runs to the bathroom to vomit. But with Demon Marguerite curled up in her womb, Lurabelle grows bold and assertive. She sends out a memo, advising that she is henceforth to be known as Evita Peron. She dresses in black leather, drinks gin and at parties has sex with all men, after which she yawns and declares, "I'm bored," as she smoothes out the leather. (The men shrivel up from loss of bone density, induced by premature osteoporosis.)

Evita Peron thirsts for excitement. She buys a large French Lobster, dresses him in a black Basque beret and names him Raoul. They become a society item, attending charity functions, chitchatting with Leona Helmsley and Donald Trump.

There is only one problem and that is Evita's Fat Slob Dad. She can't stand him and he's grown stingy. She prepares in the bathtub a mousse of Kahlua and bourbon. Fat Slob Dad laps it up and falls into a dreamless sleep. Lobster Raoul tapes shut his mouth with self-sticking magic tape. The happy couple fly away to the Canary Islands on a weeklong revel in the sun.

Fat Slob Dad tries to feed himself by drilling a hole in his stomach with a screwdriver. His death is ruled a suicide.

Evita and Lobster Raoul live it up on Evita's inheritance, until one day Lobster Raoul announces that his days are numbered, he's been out of water too long. Evita should eat him while he's still fresh.

Together they boil up a pot of water with bouquet garni. Evita eats Raoul with basmati rice, lemon asparagus and early green peas. She drinks well-chilled Pouilly Fuisse and has Poires Helene for dessert with freshly ground Columbian coffee and Armagnac.

Demon Marguerite's sabbatical is up. She vacates Evita's womb. Lurabelle Murphy is now an orphan. Her inheritance is gone. She finds work as a chambermaid at the Linus Pauling Institute where high doses of vitamin C are being used to suppress hostility in the postadolescent American male.

AFTER O'HARA AFTER MAYAKOVSKY

I have a way with words!
I will write to Senators, Congressmen,
the President! I will not be quiet!
I will send you crashing
pot-bellied Humpty Dumpty,
calling the secretaries, girls,
implying I'm too old for the job!
Don't you get it? It's against
the law, you corporate sleaze!
May your wife run off with the milkman!
Yerti da hazzare da philatsy!
Future generations will thank me!

I will not cry! I shout,
standing in the middle of the room,
my throat scraped dry.
You will be sorry! I work hard,
stay late! I'm never sick!
I'm efficient, agreeable!
I don't smoke, I don't smell!
Thank you for your interest. . .
will keep your résumé on file.
I don't want my name
in your stinking computer!
Delete, take it out!

Blood on my hands.
For God's sake, why was I crawling

on broken glass under the bed?
Oh yes, prodding the cat out
with the broom, terrified of me—
a raging beast not seen before.
Take deep breaths, equilibrate!
Cat, stop arching your back,
flailing your tail!
Can't take a little shrieking,
fair weather friend.
You don't deserve me!
Nobody deserves me!

We lean out of the window, sending
the African Violet that never blooms
onto an air conditioner glistening
with pigeon goo.
Snow falling on my face,
dirtying, stinging, wetting
the cat's electric fur on edge
like porcupine quills.
Fate, let's come to terms.
I'm a simple folk.
All I need is
some coarse black bread,
water that doesn't smell of chlorine,
a bar of soap, a change of clothes.
Has there ever been such acid snow?

REUNION

Decades since we've met and Lynn talks of Don
and nothing else. Calls him fondly by name,
not by the usual "ex." On marriage she became
mother to two motherless daughters and a son.
No babies, Don's marital stipulation,
made certain by a vasectomy. Sad tale.
I'm bored, wish for an end to this story of betrayal
with the pastor's wife, who Don claims was such fun.

I wanted to reminisce with Lynn, my friend,
generous, helpful to me, an unsure girl speaking
poor English. Abandoned by the children she raised,
the man she loved, perhaps she's been seeking
a friend before she can walk by the bend
that stops her. I'm here and listening.

REMEMBERING MY FATHER

Papa, I want to tell you that now
when I'm older than you ever were,
I still have my hair, and how often
I remember how you would look
at my pathetic skinny braids
and worry that I might become bald.
You forbade me to get a permanent.
And I wished so much to look
like the other girls in class!
I never held that against you.
I knew you wanted the best for me.
And when you left, talked into
going away by well-meaning,
foolish people who said you behaved
strangely and needed a rest. . . .
What did they expect? A man without
a job, with a family to support,
should be a regular fellow,
laughing and joking?
With all the demands on you,
you still found time to worry
about your daughter's hair.
Papa, when you finally let
these people convince you and
you went away, I went out
and got a permanent. My hair
became brittle and dull.
I cut it off and prayed that

the perm would grow out
by the time you came back.
I was going to tell you
that you were right and I knew
you would understand that
I'd wanted to experiment.
But you did not come back.

VI

LONGING

I, too, like Aphrodite, every year long for a swim in the ocean.
It is past midsummer and I have not been to the beach.
No wonder I am cranky, unhappy, pent up in the city.

Every weekend it either rains or there are social obligations.
Finally one Saturday we pack bathing suits, towels,
books, sunglasses and go, taking a chance on

the prophecy (false) of forty percent rain.
The beach is not crowded. Few radios blaring.
The tide so low, people stand in water

up to their waists and instead of jumping or swimming,
talk on the cell phones. But some things do not change.
Children build moats and castles.

A boy has dug a hole, sits in it with only his head sticking out.
Girls squeal in the water in their boyfriends' arms.
Two elderly women in baseball hats and old-fashioned

skirted swimsuits, play cards, eat homemade sandwiches,
drink iced tea from a thermos. Adolescent boys
show off in sleeveless black nylon tops,

tight matching pants, the length of knickers, looking
like the bathers in the photos of the Prohibition Era,
race into the water, splashing and yelling.

At home it takes days to get rid of the sand—
I have forgotten how it clings to everything.

NACHTKERZE

It's time, Monika said, leading us to the garden.
Nine fifteen here in Kandinsky country
at the foothills of the Alps and still light.
Watch, she said and in an instant
a bud unfurled, then another, into showy flowers,
demitasse saucers of sunshine.

A flower that flowers in the evening.
Tomorrow it will be shrunken, on the ground.
A cascade of messages switched on
at a confluence of light,
dark, temperature, moisture. . . .

A moth, so large and energetic that I wonder
if it's a hummingbird, dives in,
emerging even more invigorated, as if
newly baptized. It zigzags
to a neighbor, dives in again. . . .

Ulli tells me there are no hummingbirds here.
He used to study moths. Familiar, but can't think of
the name. Someone looks up the flower
in a reference book. *Oenothera biennis.*
Nachtkerze. Night candle.

I ask Alex to write down the name.
I always want to know the name.

Manajit asks for a shoot. Walter obligingly
brings out a spade, begins to dig.
Soon the moths are everywhere, feasting.
Their *Carpe Diem*.

WHEN I STEP OUTSIDE

and the sun is so bright
that I close my eyes,
I think of the newborn
emerging out of the warm dark,
opening eyes, crying in pain,
ignorant of what is ahead.
I, the adult, know a lot
about the future.
For instance, I predict that
when I open my eyes,
I will see cracked pavement,
a scrawny Ailanthus tree,
maybe a woman walking her dog.

THROWING AWAY THE CORSET

for Molly Peacock

My mother coming home after work,
heels clicking, body erect, nothing wiggling,
always in dark dresses, slimming, practical,
headed for the bedroom, emerging in loose
cottons, uncorseted, unhosed, feet bare.
In her seventieth year she discovered
the garter belt, threw out her corset,
by then fraying, tearing, difficult to replace
in the days of the women's young movement.
More relief came with belated acceptance
of panty hose, pants in her final year.
"I don't understand why I didn't
appreciate pants before," she would marvel,
knees apart, legs up on a table.

JULY

On a warm day, humid and noisy—
woodpeckers pounding, birds whistling,
I want to sit under a tree, shady
with large deciduous leaves,
eat cherries, spit out pits, and read a book,
stopping to rest my eyes on the sun's
progression,
the ants climbing the pits,
a yellow jacket feeling the cherries.
I want to be left alone like a dog gnawing
on a bone, a shark appearing
in the waves of a popular resort.
I don't mind the yellow jacket.
When the bowl is empty, he will fly away.

FLYING FROM ROME

The airplane glides through skies and clouds,
its motors humming steadily, reassuringly, a reminder
of the earth below.

I reread Browning's *Love in a Life: Room after room*. . .
and hope again he will find her.

NO REASON

I was feeling depressed for no reason, even
wanted to cry and did a little.

I thought of calling a long-ago friend,
but we have not been in touch and I didn't.

I sat by the window to read in the sun, but
the sky clouded over and turned grey.

I went to the playground to watch children play,
but a sign forbade entry to anyone without a child.

I stopped at the grocery to buy cherries,
but they were not in season.

I ordered coffee to take out and the woman next to me
said, "I have just come from the Veterans' hospital
where my husband is dying."

TRAVELING WITH BOOKS

Drafted to fight the Nazis, my father took a suitcase
full of books. The war would end in a few weeks,
at most a couple of months, said Our Father in the Kremlin.
Among the books was a German grammar.
Learning languages was a lifelong hobby.

Preparing for a month-long trip, I fill my suitcase
with *Martin Chuzzlewit, The Italian Renaissance,
A Sportsman's Sketches, An Anthology of Sonnets,
The Iliad,* the last four issues of *The New Yorker.*
I remove *Martin Chuzzlewit,* and *A Sportsman's
Sketches.* Not the *Iliad.* Just bought a new edition.
Should I reread *Confessions of Felix Krull?*
(Is it time for rereading, when there is so much still unread?)

What other books did my father take? Some in French,
I'm sure. The poets Tiutchev, Lermontov, Pushkin.
I see him reading after a day of manning the cannons.
Learning German to read Goethe, Mann, Schiller
in the original when he returns.

The Battle of Stalingrad over, the surviving soldiers were
ordered to assemble 300 miles north. One night my father,
worn out, hungry and resigned to dying in the freezing cold,
was asked by an officer if he could speak German.
Luck and God were with him that night.
After questioning the terrified young German soldier,
my father asked if he could stay overnight in the dugout.
With *The hell with you!* he was motioned to a corner.
Like my father, I do not travel without books.

VII

DIRT

Dirt under my fingernails.
I dig it out with a long metal file.
Going out this evening–not acceptable
to have fingernails tainted brown.

What is dirt? Under my fingernails is earth,
good brown earth for which I paid money
and which I used to transplant the aloe to a bigger pot,
flourishing wildly from a cutting Susan gave me,

that she said came from Aaron Copland's plant.
Susan is a musician and an apartment
gardener as I am. I dug, turned over the soil
with a silver-plated soup spoon.

The women in my family always
gardened, and I mean they grew dill,
potatoes, gooseberries . . . not just flowers.
It has not been given to me to have

a plot of land, but I keep on with tradition
in an apartment on the fourth floor.
I don't need or own a spade. I don't stoop,
press with one foot, lift, toss away the earth as

I remember my mother doing in Oudelnia, a suburb
of Moscow, the last place where she gardened.
What was she planting in July? I asked. At six, I knew
that this was the wrong time of the year for planting.

She was digging to hide from the enemy—
they were not going to get her winter woolen coat,
high-heeled red shoes, my father's gabardine suit
he'll wear when he comes back from Stalingrad.

MY BARE ELBOWS

"This man's knees are bare," I point to the brown leather shorts
of an Austrian tourist. "You're letting him in!"
The guard again shakes his head, barring my way.
"I'll take a quick look," says my husband, walking inside
in a short-sleeved shirt.
Outside I take out the guidebook. How could I have missed
the admonishment about bare arms?
Duomo di Milano, the second largest Gothic Cathedral in the world.
In Italy, second in size only to Saint Peter's Basilica in Rome.
Denied admittance and not even to the first, but to the second.
The Cathedral can hold 40,000 people, but there is no room for me.
"Be appropriately dressed."
Am I not appropriately dressed? Dress below the knees, high necked
collar almost touching my chin,
hose, low-heeled shoes, not even sandals with exposed toes.
Short sleeves, bare elbows.

A bus pulls up and I hear Russian spoken, my native tongue.
Soviet tourists come out,
young men with large cameras strapped to their shoulders.
"Smotri, devushka (look, a young girl/woman), put out
with the dogs!" "That's how capitalist society treats its women!"
Half-a-dozen men snap pictures of me from different angles,
some kneeling, I suppose to get in the whole cathedral.
There are no dogs, only me and the pigeons on the square.
The short-sleeved men walk past me, some saying:
"Bednaya devushka (poor young girl/woman)!"

In the hotel, before going to sleep I read in "The Travels of Marco Polo" about the shoemaker who,
while fitting a woman for a pair of slippers, viewed a woman's accidentally exposed part of her leg.
"The beauty of which excited in him a momentary concupiscence."
He recalled the words of the Gospel:
"If thine eye offend thee, pluck it out and cast it from thee;
for it is better
to enter the kingdom of God with one eye, than having two eyes
to be cast into hell fire."
The shoemaker, immediately after dismissing the woman, "with an instrument of his trade, scooped out his right eye."

In the morning I fold a lightweight silk scarf and put it inside my purse.

INTENSIVE CARE UNIT

—Nyack, 1989

A mass of tubing, orange, grey, green, black. Corrugated, wet, translucent pale blue plastic snaking into the lungs. Hands bandaged with more tubing. Four bags of fluid suspended from the ceiling. A bag at the bottom of the bed. Respirator with red numbers, heart monitor with phosphorescent green valleys and hills. Other monitors snappy blue with glowing green numbers.

Sheee, sheee, uuf—the respirator. *Beep, beep*—the monitors. The nurses come in, take a look, leave.

It's stifling in the room. My mother tries to throw off the blanket, motions with her head and eyes to lower the support stockings. Technician agrees it's unbearably hot, but isn't sure how to adjust the thermostat. We knock the cover off (Honeywell–American) and move pointers around, one black, one red. Cooler twenty minutes later. I feel useful. I've done something.

Tube in the nose to drain fluids, (tube from stomach just removed), a bag with sugar and salts, two with antibiotics. (And in the fourth? Heart medication?) Humidifier for the respiratory tube. TV with own monitor suspended from the wall, outfitted with tubes in shades of grey. *To rent this color TV, Please call Ext. 5100.* Zenith. I'm surprised it's not Toshiba or Sony. Technician comes in, adjusts, records.

Sheee, sheee, uuff, beep, beep. Who said it was the age of insects? It's the age of electronic beepers.

I look out of the window. Snow on the ground. A majestic spruce (or is it fir?), sixty feet tall at least, maybe taller. Conical, branches curving, tips pointing into the sky. Beyond the tree there are tombstones. One in front has an evergreen wreath with a large red ribbon. It's Christmas season.

I say, "Mama, this is the coldest day I can remember. The newspaper says it is not the record. In 1872 it was three degrees. Today it is eight degrees, but with the wind chill factor, twenty to thirty below zero." Being informative, but also preparing for an early departure.
My mother nods sympathetically.

In spite of all the tubing, she is alert, her green-grey eyes look into my green-grey. "Mama, did you know that Rumania is in revolt against communism?" She looks surprised. I recall she's been in the hospital for three weeks.

"Ceausescu and his wife Elena have fled. There are mass graves." My mother shakes her head in wonderment. "East Germany is no longer a communist state. There is talk of reunification." My mother's eyes widen. No, she's been in the hospital for a month, not three weeks, and before the surgery, she was too unhappy to be interested in the news. "And we have sent troops to Panama. Going after Noriega. Twenty one servicemen have been killed." She shakes her head in dismay. "Can you imagine raising a boy who gets killed like this in the prime of life?" My mother has experienced war losses: a brother killed, a husband wounded. She has lived through a son's service in Vietnam.

Six days ago, she was taken off the respirator (too soon!) and for one day she could talk. She was cheerful, optimistic. I said to her, "Mama, when you get better, you must learn English well enough to read the classics. What a misfortune you've had to read translations. A whole world of literature will open up to you." "I made many mistakes in my life," she said.

I talk about a bakery on Main Street—a recent discovery. A place my mother would have liked, with the aroma of fruit fillings and bread baking. Cakes cooling.

My mother is tired and closes her eyes. I gather my belongings, lean over the railing and kiss her on the forehead. In the doorway I look at her lying in a mass of tubing with her hair in glamorous, soft waves, white like snow in the country.

OMAHA BEACH

Depending on where you stood,
the white marble markers would shift
into different geometric designs:
parallel rows, triangles, rectangles.

Well-kept grounds, mythological sculptures,
monuments describing the war, the invasion.
Tranquil the day we were there–my husband,
I, three other Americans and a young French
couple with two children running about
whom the parents kept shushing. I expected
more tourists, but the dollar was weak and
maybe we're not a generation that visits the dead.
We walked, pausing to read the inscriptions.
Names, names, then "Only Known to God."

I don't think the soldiers minded hearing the children
laugh and shout–these were men who traveled
over the ocean to help the French. They would be
laughing and shouting themselves. Healthy, fit
young men with crew cuts in identical uniforms.
Men who did not see their children grow up, left their
wives childless, their parents with no grandchildren,
did not keep promises to marry their girlfriends.
Did not become teachers, inventors, chefs, musicians. . . .

At the beach a local man walked his dog. The surf was quiet,
the water blue. I picked up a stone, oval, smooth,
the color of sand, one end dark red, and put it in my purse.

DREAM WITH CARDBOARD SUITCASE

I can't close the suitcase, old, scratched.
Not leather, cardboard. Woolworth-bought.
The kind I used for traveling by Greyhound
after college. I sit on it.
Hot in the navy blue wool dress I made
in the high school sewing class.
The teacher was amazed at the material I brought—
Forstman wool, best quality. My mother just handed it
to me, a relic from better days.
I made covered buttons, covered buckle for the belt.
An old fashioned dress with long sleeves,
a waistline, and a lacy collar (removable).

The zipper on the Airman's flight bag that
Ann Simpson gave me for graduation is stuck.
I tug at it, trying to align the teeth. I want to leave.
It's late. Where is Ann? What happened to her?
She was one of the kindest people in my life.
She took my mother grocery shopping.
In emergencies drove us to doctors and
sometimes for a ride out of the city.
Tried to teach me to drive. There was nothing
we could do in return. It was all one way.

Ann had a baby at forty—unusual then.
She already had a daughter of thirteen.
Felix, her husband, taught forestry
at the university; in the evenings listened
to classical music on records.

One day Ann, the even-tempered,
good-natured Ann raised her voice at Felix,
cried out that here they are in their forties and
living in a pre-fab apartment along with students.
Felix was stunned. He thought they were happy.
Next day they started to look for a house.
Nothing suitable. They decided
to move to a warmer climate.

The first few years my mother and Ann
exchanged Christmas cards. By the time
I wanted to take the initiative to stay in touch,
my mother had lost their address
or they had moved again and she lost the new one.
What happened to the family?
Were they happy in New Orleans, in a house of their own?
How did the daughters' lives turn out?

I am very thirsty, keep waking up to drink
gulps of water from a plastic bottle.
There were no plastic bottles of water when
I had the cardboard suitcase. My blue dress has been
bagged and given a long time ago to the Salvation Army.
The records are dinosaurs.
I have not worn a belted dress in decades.
The suitcases are now on wheels, though they can
still be overstuffed and the zippers can stick.
All the Woolworth stores have closed.
I used to think that if I were ever in need,
I could always get a job there.
Ann would be over eighty now.

DO YOU KNOW WHO YOUR NEIGHBORS ARE?

–New York City, February 15, 2003

The city is on High Alert. Credible information of impending attacks. Be wary, but continue to live normally. "Underground" repeatedly deciphered in chatter.

Should we give up the subway, take buses, taxis, walk?
Stay indoors, not go out at all?
Mayor Bloomberg plans to continue taking the subway to work.
It is quick. It is safe. It is a bargain.

The unkempt young man sitting next to me, waiting for the train, working the crossword puzzle, smells. I analyze the smell.
Juicy fruit (sarin)? No.
Burnt almonds (cyanide)? No.
Unwashed clothes? Yes.

The rowdy teenagers in baggy pants are not patting themselves down (sign of the presence of explosives)

Do a lot of the people on the train have their eyes closed,
look as if they are sleeping or falling asleep? Don't board.
They may have been gassed.

Where is the duct tape? asks a woman.
In back, the clerk points to the back of the store.
He is misinforming the woman. The manager has helpfully put out a large cardboard box at the entrance with a sign:
"Duck tape and drop cloth are not refundable and not returnable."

How good are people at putting up plastic and sealing with duct tape? In tests some people sealed rooms in a few minutes; others took 40 minutes. Will duct tape and plastic really work?
Duct tape and plastic sheeting can offer solace and a sense of empowerment.

More solace and empowerment:

The Regional Environmental Hazard Containment Corporation sells inflatable plastic rooms costing $3,200 to $5,000.

And more (bless the entrepreneurs):

URBAN SURVIVAL KIT
Be prepared for any terror threat or emergency.

KIT INCLUDES:

NATO NBC GAS Mask, CHEMICAL SUIT & DuPont CHEM GLOVES for protection against biological/chemical pathogens, fire, & smoke inhalation.
MULTI-PURPOSE EMERGENCY TOOL to break down doors, windows or dig through debris.
120 dB PERSONAL ALARM to alert others of your location.
LONG LIFE LED FLASHLIGHT in case of power failure (it can stay on for 30 days!)
GI ISSUE CARRYING CASE (versatile & puncture proof)
EMERGENCY WATER CANISTER (connects to mask)
24 PAGE Government Survival Guide/instruction book.

(Is there no duct tape in the kit? What about radioactivity?)

Worry about a nuclear device?
Hope you're far enough away.
Confine your concerns to a cyanide or a smallpox attack.

(Can they have sex after receiving the smallpox vaccine? the most common question among the military. Yes, but advisable to wear a T-shirt.)

Should we stay in a suburban motel while the High Alert is on?

Move to a very small town to live out our days? Surely it would be safe there. Who'd want to attack when the casualties would be minimal?

My daughter calls. Wants to move back to the city. The commuting sucks. No sidewalks where they live. Can't go out for a walk with the baby in the stroller. Drive, drive, everywhere. The babysitter is lonely. *This is the worst time to be living in New York.*
People will be leaving. There will be apartments.
I don't know. I don't know. Are you at all prepared? Have a flashlight, duct tape, a battery-operated radio, bottles of water?

We are stocked up on water. In an unusual action a few years ago when we bought a new refrigerator, I read the instructions. The freezer works best if fully stocked. No food to freeze? Fill up containers with water.

And potassium iodide pills. You live not far from a nuclear station. Nuclear plants are targets.

Also theaters, hospitals, banks, schools, bridges, tunnels, parks, hotels, restaurants, churches, malls. Disneyland. Seaworld.
Circus. Shakespeare in the park.

Be on the lookout for the terrorists among us. Do you know who your neighbors are?

We are flanked by new neighbors. They travel a lot.
Receive many packages.
Call on the cell phone out on the staircase by the trash chute.
Polite, but remote.
Confine their conversation to the weather.
Quiet, virtually noiseless, really ideal neighbors.
No, we don't know who our neighbors are.

SAND IS FOR MEMBERS

> *If democracy is to prevail, public good must prevail over private interests. The question is: would the majority of people be happier with a public waterfront on the Long Island Sound or not?*
>
> –Enrique Peñalosa, *The New York Times Magazine*, June 8, 2008

NO TRESPASSING *Private Beach to Water's Edge*
–Sign in Destin, Fla. *The New York Times*, December 3, 2009

Olga and Anna, my mother's friends,
came by train to visit us on Long Island
where we rented a room for two weeks
in the house of a friend of a friend.

Good day for a visit. Our landlord had
gone away on business. My mother and I
made cheese blintzes and roasted a chicken.
Olga and Anna brought smoked herring,
dark pumpernickel, Belgian chocolates.

After lunch Olga and Anna wanted to walk
to the beach, see the ocean. Not to swim,
just walk barefoot on the sand. Nobody
on the beach, except for a man in a booth.
"Are you members?" he asked.
"This is a private beach." Our landlord
had been driving us to a much larger
noisy, crowded beach with concessions.

"Can the shoreline be private?" I asked.
"Yes, it can be and is." "Nobody is here,"
I pleaded. "Our visitors have not seen
the ocean since they fled their war-
torn country." He'll be fired if he lets us
walk on the sand. (If we jumped over the sand
into the water, we could swim? I wanted to ask.)

I convinced the guard to let us approach water,
not barefoot, but with our shoes on—
he said it would take too long to take them off.
I quickly took a picture of Olga and Anna,
then another with my mother joining them,
the ocean sunlit and foaming behind them.

My mother and I were upset, but Olga and Anna
said they were happy—they had seen the ocean.
As proof, there will be a framed photo on the bureau.

ATTACK IN TARRYTOWN

"I'm a friend, it's okay, not out to rob,
just admiring the view," I talk *sotto voce*
to the two dogs clawing me. One is a small mutt,
mostly terrier, barking and biting my ankles.
Thank God I wore pants, not the skirt and hose
as I had planned at first. The other dog is brown,
I think, Doberman, clawing at my back. Lucky for me
I wore this old puffed up North Face coat and
not the black thin wool one. "It's okay, I like you,
we're friends," I keep repeating.
The small dog begins to quiet down,
perhaps worn out by the physical exertion.

Their mistress stands silently on the porch.
"I just wanted to look at the river," I call out to her.
"I'm not afraid of dogs," I add reassuringly.
The woman commences to walk toward us.
The Doberman is jumping at my chest as I hold out
my ungloved hand poised, on the verge of stroking
its smooth short-haired forehead, just as soon as
it stops revealing its large white teeth.
"Dogs usually like me," I tell the silent woman.
"I think they must like my smell, maybe my voice–
as a rule they jump in play and lick me." Not these two.

Whether it's my soothing voice or the mistress's footsteps,
the Doberman lets out a few angry growls
and removes its paws from my chest. "I'm visiting,

decided to walk around, look at the Hudson,
the Tappan Zee Bridge. I know people don't walk here,
so why should the dogs be leashed? I understand,"
I talk hurriedly as the woman and the dogs
head for their home. I am relieved. I am whole, alive!

I came up by train. My friend had insisted that
her husband meet me at the station.
I would have preferred to walk the seven blocks
to their house instead of riding in a car.
I was early, the first guest. My friend
was brushing her hair, putting on makeup.
"I'll go for a walk in the neighborhood,
stretch my legs after the train ride," I said.
"Good idea. Enjoy the view!" she said.
A picturesque town, I thought walking up a hill,
I, the only pedestrian, cars whizzing by.
Historic. Washington fought the British here.
Then the attack as I stood admiring
the Hudson in the afternoon sun.

Inside, I take off my coat. No tears–amazing.
And if it had been torn, would I demand restitution?
Should I tell my hosts about the attack?
And ruin their party? No, I decided. Why would
they walk and not drive like their neighbors?

THINGS TO FEAR WHILE SLEEPING

Mosquitoes, fleas, rats, bats, snakes, robbers,
rapists, murderers and others entering through windows,
front door, back door, basement, skylight, toilets.

Earthquakes, meteorites, lightning striking roof,
tornado lifting house, flash floods,
falling plaster, full bladder, leg cramps.

Splinters traveling through body puncturing organs,
any non-fatal, but serious attack, such as
a heart attack (okay if fatal).

Smelling gas, burning in a fire,
being kidnapped into slavery,
cat mistaking Adam's apple for mouse.

Forgetting how to perform routine activities:
breathing in and out, swallowing saliva,
keeping tongue out of teeth's reach,
especially if they're gnashing.

Turning grey, gaining weight, acquiring wrinkles,
clogging arteries with cholesterol.

Exhibiting strange behavior: sleepwalking
on the highway, having sex with a ghost,
not hearing the alarm clock, falling out of bed.

THE PASSING CAR

I stand by the window, looking into the street, busy street
with honking taxis, crosstown buses, jaywalking pedestrians.
A red car pulls up at the entrance. A man and a woman
are inside. They don't get out, don't talk, just sit still.

As I open the door of a red convertible, I see my father
by the window. Something is going to happen. My pleasant
mood is disturbed. I thank the driver, a good-looking man
who has given me a ride from the public swimming pool.

I walk up the steps slowly. My legs are heavy, there's
a contraction in my stomach. My father watches
as I go to the bathroom to hang up the wet bathing suit
and towel. When I come out he asks: "Who was that man?
Anyone we know?" My father's blue eyes, now almost
colorless with hardly any pupil, are fixed on me.
He's smoking a Lucky Strike. I think he'd like to hit me.

I can't lie. I tell him a stranger offered me a ride.
I had just missed the bus and the next one wouldn't be
coming for forty minutes. No, I haven't been accepting
rides regularly, this is only the second time (actually,
the third). My mother is somewhere in the background,
not saying anything. I sense her anxiety.

In my room I take off the red shorts and put on a skirt.
I look at my face in the mirror. It's very burnt, the skin
peeling on the nose from a former burn. My hair has
a greenish tinge from the chlorine. I can smell it on my arms.

I go out for a walk. I think of leaving home. At fifteen
I look older. That's what the man said. He thought I was
at least eighteen. I could go to San Francisco and get
a job as a waitress. My parents are having a difficult time.
My father isn't working. Something happened. People are
coming around, telling him he should go away for a rest.

My mother is looking for a job. She relies on my help.
After school I take my brother and sister to the playground.
I try to find them friends. We have recently moved here
and know hardly anyone. Next week my brother and sister
are turning four and I'm organizing a birthday party.
Twenty children are coming with their mothers.

I walk for hours. I should know better than accept rides
from strangers. Why am I so hurt and angry? It would help me
to cry, but I can't. My father is trying to make an important
decision. He hardly sleeps or eats, just smokes. He's lost weight.
He's exhausted. He's not going to make the right decision.

It's dark when I come home. My mother is sitting
on the front porch. She tells me there's chicken and rice
on the stove. She's glad I'm back. I turn the light on
in the kitchen and start eating the chicken. I'm very hungry.
Everything will be all right. This unhappiness will pass.
From the window I see my father smoking on the back porch.

When I walk away from the window, the red car with the man
and woman inside is still parked in front of our building.
Later when I close the window, it's not there anymore.

ON A TRAIN ALONG THE HUDSON RIVER

Has there ever been a more handsome sight than the Hudson River?
I have such luck today, a seat by the window.

Water, water, then suddenly a long narrow stretch of
green rises up, an alligator-shaped island–
the snout, the knobby grass, bumps on the skin,
a peninsula jutting out, on the end a run-down cottage,
more islands with erector-set constructs in dark red,
one with a house, a church, maybe our own American castle.

The haze gives way to an overcast sky with the sun
breaking through. My problems recede: the broken
vacuum cleaner, the still unknown results of
a medical test, the mysterious cooling off from a friend.
Across the aisle a woman crochets something blue.
(A baby blanket?) Stops, counts, unravels, starts again.
In back a woman on the cell phone tells someone
she'll be there by 6:30 and is it known
about the surgery yet? No, not yet.

A young man walks by with a cardboard tray carrying
something from the snack bar. Earlier he helped me put up
my suitcase on the rack. His head is shaved, except
for a stripe of hair in the middle. I take out
my dark rye, cheese, tomato and lettuce sandwich.
The man at the ticket counter advised me to bring
my own sandwich. I take big swallows of tap water in
an Evian bottle, munch on slices of cucumber,

for dessert an apple and pecans. The woman in back is
eating something smelly. Meatloaf I decide, and wish
for some myself, along with mashed potatoes and peas.

I'm barely conscious of the quiet monotone that propels
the train forward, changing to dull thumping
going over a bridge. Across the river another train–
red, green, yellow, black cars like a necklace of
colored macaroni my daughters used to present me with
in kindergarten. Whistles exchanged in greeting.
A bit of music. I read a stanza of "A Song of Myself,"
then stare at the water. Nothing bothers me.
Even the lonely graffiti that looks like crooked
pyramids seem to enliven the bleak grey underpass.

Bulky, unwieldy, overgrown mountains,
solid, not bothering anyone; the nuclear plant
projecting like a two-headed mosque,
just a baby, but already causing discord.
The river is not overused. An occasional barge,
boat, marina. Two men fishing, bare-chested,
very red, on their heads Mets hats.
The white crests look like the handkerchief tops
poking out of the well-dressed men's jackets.
Nobody swimming.

The river beckons: *Come to me*, and the cables
and trees lean, the branches bend, almost touching the water.
The train stops, the announcer says there is
a disabled train in front. Earlier someone told me
the passenger trains are late because the same tracks
are used for freight and they're hard on the rails.
I don't mind the delay. It may be a long time before I take a ride
along the Hudson again. And, like the trees and the cables,
I lean to the window to get closer to the river.

LISTENING TO THE THUNDER

When it thundered, mother
    would draw the drapes, sit silently
        away from the windows.

She would ask us to turn off the radio,
    hang up the phone, stop washing dishes,
        get out of the shower.

She once saw a man struck
    by lightning. He was standing
        under a tree holding his son's hand.

When I hear thunder, I turn off
    the computer, sit on the sofa, drink
        coffee and listen to the thunder.

www.ingramcontent.com/pod-product-compliance
Lightning Source LLC
Chambersburg PA
CBHW071718040426
42446CB00011B/2115